DATE DUE

			PRINTED IN U.S.A.

E

"Borders"
Montclair
9/19/98

DECORATIVE PAPER

Andrea Maflin

with Simon Laity

Photography by Carl Warner

Trafalgar Square Publishing

*To my beloved father, whose strength and faith in me
have given me the courage and belief to achieve my ambitions.*

First published in the United States of America in 1995 by
Trafalgar Square Publishing, North Pomfret, Vermont 05053

Printed and bound in Hong Kong

First published in Great Britain in 1995 by
Conran Octopus Limited, 37 Shelton Street, London WC2H 9HN

Art Editor: Alison Fenton
Commissioning Editor: Louise Simpson
Project Editor: Alison Bolus
Production Controller: Mano Mylvaganam
Illustrator: Andrea Maflin

Library of Congress Catalog Card Number: 95-60029

ISBN 1-57076-027-6

Typset by Richard Proctor

CONTENTS

Introduction

ON GLANCING THROUGH this book you would be wrong to assume that there are many tools and skills needed in order to complete these projects successfully. In fact, most of the tools can be found at home, and those few materials not readily available from your local stationers or art supply shop can be obtained from the suppliers listed at the end of the book. As for the skills, you will find most of the projects involve no more than tracing, painting (be it with dyes, tea or bleach), cutting and sticking. Anything slightly more complicated – such as applying metal leaf – is explained in foolproof detail; and the specially designed templates at the end of the book will ensure you have all the motifs you need.

I cannot stress too much that there is no right or wrong method of completing any project. When I make a mistake, I don't despair: I prefer to look at how the goal posts of the project can be moved to accommodate my most recent 'feature'!

If you are not bowled over by a project as shown, take a second look, thinking how it could be adapted to suit your own taste or the taste of the lucky recipient of this special gift. Don't be afraid to add your own trait, be it from a chance slip of the brush or a mused alteration of the colours chosen. Above all, though, have fun.

TOP LEFT Once you have experimented with the various decorative paper techniques outlined on pp. 14-19, use some of the plentiful supply of decoupage motifs on pp. I-IV to design your own wrapping paper, cards and gift tags. Then try out your newly-learned skills on this splendid Celebration Photograph Album.

TOP RIGHT This beautiful autumnal sewing box is a combination of two of the projects outlined in this chapter on containers: the Torn Paper Heart Box and the Autumn Leaf Tray. Always keep an open mind and an open eye with regard to my projects, and be prepared to adapt ideas and decoration to suit your own tastes.

BOTTOM LEFT The three clocks included in this chapter could not be more different, and yet each is stunning in its own way. The Seashore Clock shown here is a colourful, evocative reminder of sun, sea and sand; the Gentleman's Outfitter's Clock is simplicity and sartorial elegance itself, with its understated colouring and stylish motifs; finally, the Bejewelled Silver Clock is luxurious and romantic with its glowing jewels and gleaming metal leaf.

BOTTOM RIGHT The importance of a frame should never be under-estimated. I have included two picture frames in this chapter - one in cool pale blue and white and the other in sophisticated sepia and black - as well as the Gilded Script Mirror shown here. Many of the decorative motifs supplied on pp. I-XII would transform the plainest frame into a work of art.

Colour Mixing

YOU WILL NEED

SUNFLOWER YELLOW DYE

PINK DYE

TURQUOISE DYE

BLUE INK

BLACK INK

COLOUR IS something we take for granted, and we often fail to notice just how glorious the colours of nature are. Mixing your own colours is very rewarding and great fun, and to help you I have produced here a simple and easy-to-follow guide to which you can keep returning while you make some or all of these decorative paper projects. I have deliberately not provided

SUGARED ALMOND PINK

90% WATER

10% PINK

PURPLE

60% BLUE INK

40% PINK

SUNFLOWER YELLOW

90% YELLOW

10% PINK

BURNT ORANGE

50% YELLOW

50% PINK

a colour wheel, because the colours of the cold water fabric dyes I use (turquoise, sunflower yellow and fuchsia pink) and the fountain pen inks (blue and black) do not combine together in the way of a traditional wheel, and it would be misleading to suggest otherwise. This is my own way of mixing the vast array of colours I use from just 3 dyes and 2 inks. Don't feel restricted to my suggestions, but use them as a guiding arm, trying out your own experiments along the way.

I have given percentages for the amounts of inks and dyes needed to produce each colour, so you will find it almost effortless to achieve the colours shown (although please note that the printing process alters the colours slightly from my originals).

LILAC BLUE

80% BLUE INK

20% PINK

SEA GREEN

90% TURQUOISE

10% YELLOW

TERRACOTTA

50% YELLOW   40% PINK

10% BLACK INK

OLIVE GREEN

70% YELLOW   10% BLACK INK

10% TURQUOISE   10% PINK

MINT GREEN

80% TURQUOISE

15% YELLOW   5% PINK

RED

60% PINK

40% YELLOW

Papers

BEING SUCH AN integral part of everyday life, paper is all too often taken

for granted. Try to detach yourself from the daily acts of reading and using

paper and marvel instead at its versatility. Some papers are delicate, such

as bark paper and filmy tissue, whilst others are very tough, such as the

corrugated paper, which is given considerable strength from a succession

The subtle shades of the dressmaking pattern, tea-bag, gold script and fibrous papers are beautifully offset by the gleaming gold tissue. Note the intricate texture of the imitation crocodile paper and the colourful swirls of the handmade marbled paper.

of fine ribs. Some have a rough, rustic surface; others have a satin smooth finish just asking to be written on.

All the papers you can find will be enhanced by the treatments explained in this book. Touch and feel each paper, appreciating its qualities, and don't hesitate to crease it, crumple it, fold it or tear it. Use the ideas demonstrated in this book and transform today's enticing papers into tomorrow's works of art

The stunning array of colours is matched only by the wide variety of textures, from filmy tissues and soft handmade papers to rough crêpe paper and tough, fine-ribbed, corrugated sheets.

TOOLS

1 Scissors
2 2.5 cm/1 in and 5 cm/2 in paintbrushes
3 Nylon paintbrush
4 Lino block
5 Lino-cutting tool
6 Self-healing cutting mat
7 Scalpel
8 Pencil
9 Sandpaper and block
10 Ruler
11 Motifs
12 Eraser
13 Dressmaking pins
14 Masking tape
15 Clear adhesive tape
16 Paper clips
17 Palette
18 Artist's brushes
19 Bradawl
20 Ruling pen
21 Phillips screwdriver
22 Flat screwdriver
23 Compass

MATERIALS

1 Raffia
2 Clear satin varnish
3 White emulsion
4 Applicator for 5
5 Car body filler (2-part)
6 Diluted white household glue
7 Books of transfer metal leaf
8 Lampshade rings
9 Multiple-density fibreboard (MDF)
10 Multi-purpose glue

11 Circular mirror
12 Plain lampshade
13 Tea bags for tea staining
14 Jewels
15 Glass
16 Clock mechanism and hands
17 Plain picture frames
18 Hinges and catches
19 Mount board
20 Double-sided sticky tape

21 Cold water fabric dyes
22 Black marker
23 Candle
24 Spray varnish
25 Acrylic paints
26 Fountain pen inks
27 Diluted bleach
28 Aerosol adhesive

Techniques

EACH PROJECT uses these simple techniques to generate impressive effects from a few basic concepts. Use the illustrations as a stimulus for your individual creations, changing any colours you want and combining different effects with various background colours.

There are few rules written in stone with regard to paper work, but it is worth reading pp. 18–19 for guidelines on safe and careful cutting, controlled tearing and effective glueing and taping.

WAXING

1 This basic resist technique is both simple and effective. Using a white candle, mark the paper with your chosen pattern, then brush over a strong colour wash and marvel at the sudden appearance of your hidden work. The wax will prevent any liquid from soaking through to the paper, and so remain white, creating a batik effect.

BLEACHING

2 Dilute 1 part household bleach with 3 parts water, and apply to coloured papers. (This 3:1 dilution is what is meant when 'diluted bleach' is referred to in the text.) Use an acrylic brush, because the bristles will drop out of a natural one. The bleach removes the colour pigments from the paper, reverting the treated areas to the base colour of the paper. The results appear within seconds, and the effect is fascinating. Brushing, dripping, spotting and splashing each create their own effect, with the bleach bleeding gently into each colour.

Even when diluted, bleach is a liquid to be handled with great care: avoid splashes to skin and clothes.

TEA STAINING

3 Add 3 tea bags to a cupful of boiling water and leave to stew. This creates a strong natural dye, which turns a photocopy into an 'ancient manuscript' within minutes. After applying the first coat, and allowing it to dry, splash the mixture around a bit without worrying about missing patches, thereby creating a brush stroke effect. The more coats you apply, the darker the colour.

GILDING

4 Transfer metal leaf (also known as gold leaf) is a relatively inexpensive way of producing a most luxurious finish. It is sold in books of 25 sheets, and a single book would be enough to complete all the projects in this book.

Coat your paper with a very thin layer of varnish or diluted glue, then place the metal leaf (cut to your required shape) on top, smoothing out any air bubbles, and gently peel off the waxed paper backing. It will dry within minutes. Any errors need to be corrected almost immediately, by scraping off the leaf. Once dry, your only repair option is to place more leaf over the top of the misplaced piece.

Two carefully applied coats of varnish will protect it from wear, but it will always remain slightly delicate.

COLOUR MIXING

5 All the colours used in the projects are formed from the following dyes and inks: fuchsia pink, sunflower yellow and turquoise cold water fabric dyes, and black and blue fountain pen inks. The dyes (which come in powder form) and inks can be mixed with each other to form a wide variety of shades, and 'recipes' for the main colours I use are given on pp. 8 – 9. A palette is a very useful tool to hold your various experiments in colour, but plain white saucers will do just as well.

Try to restrict yourself – as I have done – to just a few colours, and see how varied your colour palette will be; and don't be afraid to try your own variations on my 'recipes'. A little more of one colour and a little less of another might make just the colour you want.

Experiment, too, with watering down a colour to achieve varying tones: burnt orange can be turned into any shade from flame orange to soft peach simply by the addition of increasing amounts of water.

You may find it takes a few goes to get the colour just right, but this is all part of the learning process, and many wonderful colours are stumbled upon in this way.

When applying your colours to your chosen papers, wash over with generous amounts of colour, using an artist's brush or a 2.5 cm/1 in paintbrush. Don't worry if the paper wrinkles with the wetness; it will tighten up as it dries.

BRUSHING

6 The brushes listed in the tools section of each project were the brushes I used for the work, but you may well be able to achieve good results with whatever you have to hand. All the basic brushwork – for colouring and pasting – can be done with any household paintbrush (5 cm / 2 in for large areas; 2.5 cm / 1 in for smaller). In addition you will need a fine artist's brush for detailed work and a nylon brush for bleach work. Shown here are a nylon brush (top left), a 2.5 cm / 1 in brush (top right) and an artist's brush (bottom).

Where a project involves more than one activity using similar materials (e.g. emulsion, colour washes, tea or glue – all of which are water based) only one brush is listed. Wash and dry your brush thoroughly between different tasks.

STRETCHING

7 Crêpe paper is a remarkably flexible paper that will expand up to three times its width when wetted. When applying crêpe paper you must wet it thoroughly on one side with diluted glue, and gently lift and stretch it as you apply it to the desired surface. There will almost certainly be air bubbles trapped underneath; use the pasting brush to expel these and to smooth the paper firmly into place.

NOTE ON MEASURING

Where measurements are required for constructing projects, both metric and imperial are given. Please follow only one system, as the two are not inter-changeable.

7

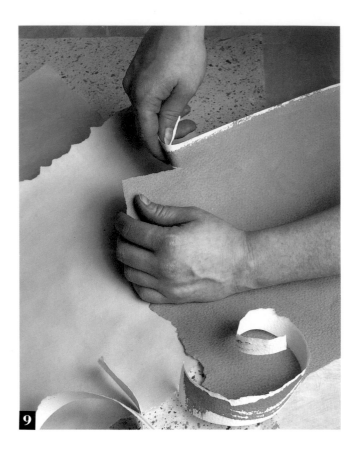

CUTTING

8 A scalpel has distinct advantages over a pair of scissors when you are cutting thick, inflexible sheets (e.g. card) and freehand curves. A wad of newspaper will protect your surface adequately – and at no cost – but will need regular replacing. For repeated use it might be worth buying a self-healing cutting mat, which magically 'mends' itself after each cut.

When using a scalpel, always make sure that the hand holding the paper is not likely to suffer if the blade slips. The illustration shows me cutting a freehand curve for the bin project; the line of the cut is curving away from my hand.

Always use a sharp blade, because the extra force required to make a blunt blade cut the paper or card increases the likelihood of slipping and subsequent injury.

TEARING

9 Papers have varied grain structures depending on their method of construction. Woven and laid are the two main varieties available from a stationer. (Laid paper has the slightly ribbed surface.) More elaborate and decorative papers, as used in many of the projects, are often found to have visible grain. This greatly affects the way in which they can be ripped. The illustration shows how I am tearing along the grain, following a relatively straight line with little effort. Ripping across the grain, also shown, is a much more haphazard affair, with straight lines quite difficult to achieve unless you use a straight edge to tear against. Some papers can be folded to help obtain a clean tear, but experiment on a little patch first: a few of the thicker-grained papers are sometimes too brittle for this.

DOUBLE-SIDED TAPING

10 This tape is not cheap, but it is invaluable in certain circum-stances. It comes on a roll with a shiny backing surface which is peeled off when the first side has been stuck down, revealing a thin layer of very sticky adhesive. It sticks to almost anything (including scissors), so it is best cut with a scalpel. It needs to be used wherever glue would cause warping of thicker cards or unacceptable wrinkling of thinner papers. If using several adjacent strips, ensure that there is no overlap or gap between them, thereby preventing unwanted ridges from appearing through the paper. Don't try to cut strips to the exact length because this will call for perfect application first time. You cannot reposition the tape once stuck, so it is better to leave an overlap at the ends and trim if off with a scalpel.

GLUEING

11 White household glue (also known as polyvinyl acetate or PVA) is my work-horse from the variety of adhesives available today. It is cheap, versatile, dries quickly, has no pungent odours, can be readily diluted with water and is about as safe to use as a glue can be. I use it diluted 1 part glue to 3 parts water in my projects, and this dilution is what is meant when 'diluted glue' is mentioned in the text. Stronger dilutions, or neat glue, are specified where required.

Stir the glue before use, and wash your brush afterwards. The glue becomes a clear, moisture-resistant layer when dry.

When pasting paper, always brush over the edges on to your surface to ensure the edges are completely covered. There is nothing more likely to let a project down than peeling edges and rough joins.

NOTE ON USING THE TEMPLATES

If the designs provided at the back of the book are not large enough for your project, you will need to enlarge them on a photocopier. If a repeat design is required, you will need to make same-size copies. Unless you have a photocopier of your own, it is worth reading a project's instructions right through before you start so that you know in advance if any copying is required.

If the template you want to use is backed by one you want for another project, trace off the relevant one with pencil on to tracing paper, turn the paper over and scribble firmly on the reverse of all the traced lines, then reverse the paper again, place it on your chosen paper and go over the outline again. When you lift up the tracing paper the image will be left on your paper.

STATIONERY

IF, LIKE ME, you are a dreadful letter writer and are always late sending birthday cards, then take a tip from me: people are so pleased to receive personalized, handmade offerings that they forgive your sins immediately! Make a good selection of cards and papers and decorate a generous amount of notepaper, and then you will be ready for every occasion. You might even find that, with this ready supply, you send your cards and write your letters on time in future!

When a special occasion demands a present instead of just a card, combine some of the decorative paper techniques shown here to adorn a splendid photograph album.

All forms of stationery can be transformed using attractive motifs, some inks and dyes and a little know-how.

All Wrapped Up

THE COLLECTION of motifs taken from ancient wood carvings

forms a unique and simple theme for making all the

paraphernalia that has become an all but essential, yet

fun, part of giving for many. Whilst it may take slightly longer

than simply stocking up with wrapping paper, ribbons and

gift tags from the shops, I liken it to cooking: a little extra time and effort

in the kitchen produces an outstanding result with greater flavour! The

motifs supplied are copied on a photocopier and washed as easily as

adding the salt and pepper! The resulting visual feast of citrus colours and detail increases the pleasure of giving and receiving.

The gift wrap sheets are simple and great fun to compose, and you can use the motifs provided in this book or choose your own images. In addition to colour washing, try using bleach for an unusual highlighting effect, or for an all-over patterning on the tissue papers. Adorn the gift tags with bright ribbons for a great finishing touch.

The cards, gift wrap and labels can be designed to complement each other, to elaborate on a theme, or be made in vibrant clashing colours.

YOU WILL NEED

MATERIALS
*Aerosol adhesive · A2 sheet white paper ·
inks and cold water fabric dyes of your
choice · bleach · coloured tissue papers ·
white crêpe paper · thick watercolour
paper (300 gsm) · double-sided sticky
tape · wool or ribbon*

TOOLS
*Motifs from pp.I - IV · saucer or palette ·
artist's paintbrush · jar · nylon brush ·
scissors · scalpel*

1 Photocopy the motifs on pp.I - IV. Rip out each image separately from the photocopy. Avoid cutting them out because the edges may become visible on the later photocopies. Glue the motifs on to the white paper, randomly mixing the orientation of each motif, duplicating any favourites you may have. Take several photocopies of this 'master' artwork on a photocopier capable of handling A2. Mix a combination of inks and/or fabric dyes (see pp. 8 – 9 for guidance). Wash individual papers all over with the colours and allow to dry for 10 minutes.

2 Washing one of the papers with black ink might seem rather strange, but you will still be able to spot the images behind the ink. To bring the images out of obscurity from behind their different colours, allow them about 10 minutes to dry, then brush them with some diluted bleach (using the nylon brush). Within seconds they should come to life. With most colours the reaction should be instant with high contrast, whilst others merely fade away to a lighter shade upon application of the bleach.

3 The tissue papers are simpler still: using the same bleach mixture, brush on any repeating pattern. With the bleach taking many seconds to react on some colours, it can sometimes be difficult to see where the last line was made. In this situation, you can either wait for the marks to appear or decide not to care too much, applying the next regardless, adding individuality to the work. Ensure that as you treat successive papers with the bleach you don't place them on top of each other (or the carpet) before they are dry.

4 The crêpe paper has been used to make ribbons. Wash it with several different colours side by side, stretching it across the grain slightly as you do so. Hang until dry (30 minutes). Mark several rows, a couple of centimetres apart, of successive bleach spots down each colour panel. It is interesting to see how each spot spreads along the grain of the paper, but not across it. When dry, cut out with scissors to form strips of ribbon.

The gift tags and the cards are both arrived at via very similar methods. Cut out any spare motifs and wash with colours and then bleach as required. Stick them, together with any spare tissue papers, on to the thick watercolour paper, using spray adhesive for the lighter papers and double-sided tape for the photocopy paper. Trimming the finer detail round the edge of the gift tags can be done cautiously with a scalpel, as can the hole. Finally, double up a piece of wool or ribbon, feed it through the hole from behind, loop it through itself and tighten it.

Personalized Notepaper

IN THE NOW heady days of perfectly typeset letterheads generated on computers, what better present could you give than a customized letterhead based upon a hobby or interest, produced from a stamp carved in traditional style? Before putting pen to paper add your own unique touch to the paper on which you will write. With a heart for a love letter or a witch on her broom for Hallowe'en invitations, you can graphically set the mood for the reader upon first glimpse. Decorate sheets of paper as you need them, or make wonderful presents by printing off boxfuls of paper and envelopes adorned with your loved one's favourite motif.

Cutting your design out on a lino board will probably take you straight back to school art classes, and all the fun you had creating your own lino prints. It may no longer be child's play, but it will still be very rewarding.

The left-hand and centre ducks were printed on white paper, and then had colour washed over them; the duck on the right was printed over a colour wash.

YOU WILL NEED

MATERIALS
*Acrylic paint in various colours ·
watercolour paper*

TOOLS
*Pencil · original drawings or printed
motifs · tracing paper · lino board ·
lino-cutting tool · saucer or palette ·
artist's paintbrush*

1 With a pencil, draw your pattern
straight on to the smooth side of the
lino. Should you prefer, you can trace a
motif from the back of the book or any
other source. Using a lino-cutting tool, cut
the lino on the smooth side either on or
around the pencil marks, depending on
the thickness of the line required.
Remember that the cuts will not be shown
– it is the remaining lino areas that will
make the pattern. Avoid cutting too deep,
since you will break through into the
hessian backing layer. Be very careful,
keeping the fingers of your other hand
back behind the cutting edge as you cut.

2 When you are happy with the design
on the lino, wash a base colour on to
the paper using watered-down acrylic
paint (mixed approx. 2 parts water to 1
part acrylic, depending on the thickness of
paper used; if the mix is too weak the

paper will wrinkle). Allow 20 minutes or
so to dry. Add a tiny drop of water to some
acrylic paint, smoothing the texture of it
slightly, and paint with a brush on to the
desired areas of the lino print.

3 Press the lino print on to the paper
on top of the existing background
colour. Lift it off to reveal a work of art
that can be repeated time and again.
Experiment with different background
colours, combining several at a time. Try
using weak colours to create a watermark
on the paper.

Always remember to wash the ink out
of the grooves of the lino-cut before it
dries in order to get clean, sharp prints
each time.

3

Celebration
Photograph Album

I CONSIDER FAMILY photo albums to be very special, becoming increasingly precious over the course of one's life. For this reason I feel they should be given the personal and cherished treatment they deserve and that befits the priceless sentimental value of their contents. Making the entire album from scratch is beyond the realms of my patience, so I have adorned the bindings of a quality album (superb handmade ones are available as well as the mass-produced ones from stationers) with a combination of the various techniques described earlier in the book. The result is a colourful collection of many different paperworking methods.

Fill this album with your own family photographs, or give it to someone special as a birthday, wedding or christening present that will always be treasured.

Old favourites can now be treasured inside an album made from the simplest of techniques, each working from the templates on p. V.

YOU WILL NEED

MATERIALS

Blue and black inks · A2 sheet of layout paper, torn into 4 smaller sheets · bleach · 1 sheet thick cartridge paper (130 gsm) · candle · pink and yellow cold water fabric dyes · brown paper · 1 sheet natural paper (handmade, sugar or recycled) · 1 sheet transfer metal leaf · white household glue · A4 photograph album · clear satin varnish

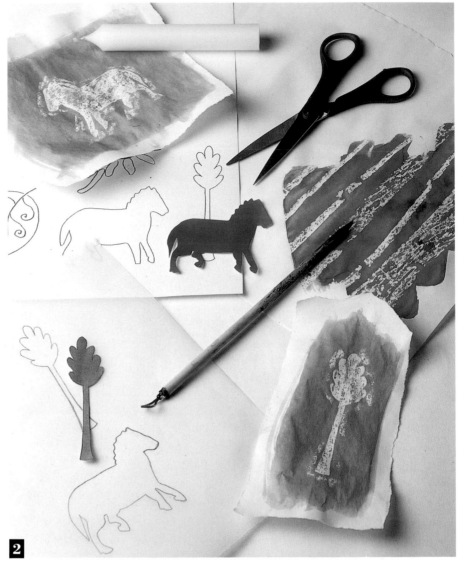

TOOLS

2.5 cm/1 in paintbrush · jar · ruling pen · dish · artist's paintbrush · pencil · motifs on p.V · tracing paper · nylon brush · scissors · palette · ink pen · 2.5 cm/1 in paintbrush

1 Wash 1 small sheet of layout paper with an ink solution made from 2 parts blue to 1 part black, and allow it to dry. Dip your ruling pen into some diluted bleach, tap off any excess, and then write or draw any pattern on the dark sheet (making sure your work surface will not be damaged by any bleach soaking through). Leave it to dry. Rinse and dry your ruling pen to prevent rusting.

Reserve a little of the dark ink mixture and dilute the rest with an equal amount of water. Rinse your brush, then wash another sheet of paper with this weaker solution and allow it to dry. Keep what is left of this solution to one side. Trace off, or copy, the flower on p.V and use a fine artist's brush and the reserved dark ink to paint the centre of each flower. Finally, bleach the leaves and the stem away using the nylon brush and the diluted bleach.

2 Trace off the tree, horse, etc. from p.V (or any motif of your own choice). Transfer these outlines on to the cartridge paper and then cut them out. Place these thick paper shapes (the horse is shown coloured in the photo just for clarity) under the third sheet of layout paper. Rub each raised image with the candle on its side, making sure you are working on a flat surface so that the image gets waxed evenly. Try to ensure that your wax does not go far beyond the outlines otherwise you will lose the shape's definition. Now brush over each waxed

3

image with the light blue ink wash.

Divide your fourth sheet in half, and on one half draw some rough lines with your candle – as thick or as thin as you want. Mix a terracotta wash from your dyes (see p. 9) and brush it over the top to reveal your wax lines.

3 Choose a favourite poem or song and transcribe it in ink on to the brown paper. Trace or copy one of the leaf motifs on p.V (or one of your own) on to your choice of natural paper.

Finally, wash the remaining half sheet of layout paper with the terracotta wash, then cut out a star from the metal leaf; leave it on its backing paper until you are ready to apply it. When the paper has dried, brush some diluted glue in the centre to cover an area larger than the star, then gently press the star in place and remove the backing.

Decide on a pleasing arrangement of the papers – mixing colours and patterns to your liking. Now coat the front of your album with a strong (1:1) mixture of glue and water, and coat the backs of your prepared papers too. Then gently stick them all down, being very careful not to get glue on to the front of the colour-washed papers, as it will leach the colour out. (Keep some tissues handy in case!)

Finally, coat the album front with a thin wash of clear satin varnish.

CONTAINERS

FROM DELICATE COLOURINGS on tiny boxes to
bold adornments on teatime trays, it is such fun to
revive everyday items and to rescue them from
dreariness, giving them a new lease of life. The
containers included in this chapter are all very
different in form and content – an oval glass
vase, an angular wastebin, a lidded box and an
elegant tray – but all have been transformed
through the application of paper shapes.

When you know how simple it is to turn
workaday containers into items of beauty, you
will shop with a wider outlook on merchandise.
Buy shapes that please you, then choose some
unusual, eye-catching paper and set to work.

*Notice how the leaves from the tray project on p.46 have been used
to transform another everyday item, in this case a sewing box.*

Tissue Layers Vase

GLASS IS A WONDERFUL, captivating material: it can be strong and durable or delicate and fragile; it can be intricately worked or left with pure simple lines; it can be shimmeringly clear or a deep Venetian blue. In this case a beautiful oval vase has been transformed into a contemporary – yet still useful – piece of art, by no more than the careful cutting and application of some scintillating metallic paper shapes. The elegant result has the added attraction of the design being visible from both the front and the rear.

YOU WILL NEED

MATERIALS
Metallic-finished tissue papers · ready-mixed goldsize · glass vase

TOOLS
Scissors · dish · artist's paintbrush · cotton bud · white spirit

1 Lay out your tissue papers (I chose ones in gold, bronze and dark silver). Despite their metallic coatings they are quite robust and can be handled without due concern for creasing. Cut out a generous selection of shapes so that you have lots of scope when planning your design. I opted for oblongs, ovals and wriggling squiggles; if you are unsure about your own shapes, experiment with scraps first.

2 When you are satisfied with your design, brush the size thinly over a small area of the vase and then leave it for 5 minutes to get tacky. Press a tissue shape on and pat it with a dry brush to remove any air bubbles. If your design involves layering your shapes, brush some more size over the base layer, leave it to go tacky then press on the second layer. When the shapes are complete, brush over them with more size to saturate them completely. Leave to dry.

Any size left on the glass is quite noticeable, so after 30-40 minutes, just before the size has completely hardened, clean off any excess around the shape using a cotton bud dipped in white spirit. Do not clean right up to the edges because you will need to maintain a small overlap to seal the papers.

Your vase is now fit for use. When the outside gets wet, pat it dry gently rather than rubbing it fiercely, and never use any abrasive cleaner on it!

Colour-wave Wastebin

THE PRECISION AND exactness of this angular bin are softened in this project through the careful application of a few colour-washed papers. Within minutes the harsh lines have been mellowed by overlapping tones of sugared almond pink, burnt orange, sea green, olive, soft sage and peppermint. The feminine characteristics that the project is given through this choice of colours are offset slightly by the mirror-image patterning of the grains in the veneer-style papers.

This is a very simple and speedy project, involving no more than cutting and sticking, and so you will have the added satisfaction of a quick result. Whilst I find it most satisfying to make all the components of a project, I wouldn't recommend attempting to construct the bin yourself unless you are familiar with woodwork. A trip to the shops or the renovation of an old bin will be much quicker.

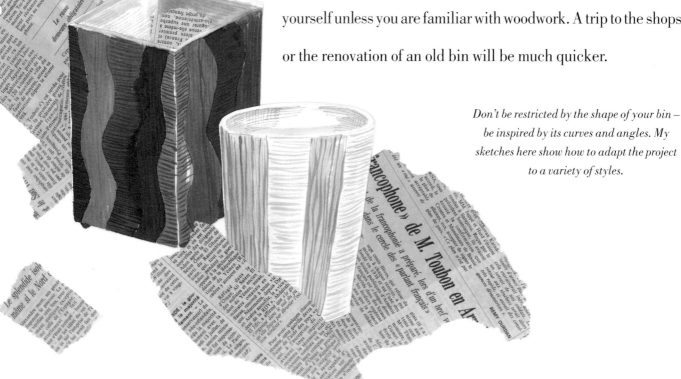

Don't be restricted by the shape of your bin –
be inspired by its curves and angles. My
sketches here show how to adapt the project
to a variety of styles.

YOU WILL NEED

MATERIALS
Bin · white emulsion · white, yellow and red acrylic paints · wood veneer paper (comes on a paper backing) · turquoise, pink and yellow cold water fabric dyes · black ink · white household glue · clear satin varnish

TOOLS
2.5 cm/1 in brush · sandpaper · scissors · palette · straight edge · scalpel · jar

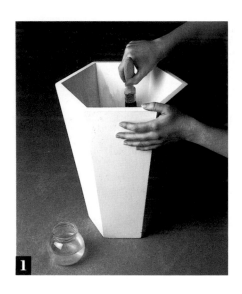

1 Paint your chosen bin all over with emulsion. Leave it to dry, sand it down lightly and paint again. Mix your acrylic paints (1 part white to 1 part yellow, plus a tiny drop of red) then use this mixture to paint the inside of the bin, starting from the bottom and working upwards, and using a wet brush to dilute the colour. Finish off with continuous brush strokes from the bottom to the top. Paint the top edge, or rim, too. Don't worry if any paint goes on to the outside of the bin as this will soon be covered with paper.

2 Cut out 6 pieces of paper, each large enough to cover one side of the bin, plus a generous overlap. Cut 3 pieces across the grain of the paper and 3 pieces along the grain. Also cut out a slightly oversized piece for the base.

(If your bin is square, cut 4 pieces of paper – 2 along the grain and 2 across. If your bin has an uneven number of sides it might be best to keep all the veneer grains in the same direction and to rely on the different colours for contrast.)

Mix your colour washes from the dyes and inks specified, and following the

recipes on pp. 8 – 9. (Add extra water to olive green to get sage green.) Wash each piece of paper with a different colour, and leave them to dry. Finally, lay each piece in turn over one side of the bin, and pinch or rub creases along the top, bottom and sides to create an outline of the bin side.

(I chose muted shades for my bin but you could equally well choose 6 bright colours, or 6 shades of 1 colour, or even opt for a minimalist combination of black and white.)

4 Use diluted glue to stick your first piece of paper on to the bin, but leave the curved overlap free of glue. Stick on the adjacent piece that will be overlapped (remembering to use the opposite grain direction of paper) and then carefully paste the overlap and stick it down. Do this neatly because any glue spilt on to the colour-washed veneer of the overlapped piece may leach the colour out, leaving patches of base tone. Repeat this process round the bin, alternating the grain directions, until all the sides are covered with papers. When the sides are

3 On a flat, protected surface cut the top, bottom and left-hand edge of each piece of paper using a scalpel against a straight edge. For each right-hand edge, cut a gently waving freehand curve. It is better not to follow a pre-drawn pencil line as this tends to make your cutting action awkward and the subsequent cut rather jagged. There is no need to try to achieve consistency between the different curves. Indeed it is the differing nature of the freehand curves which breaks the uniformity of the bin and softens the harsh angles.

dry, turn the bin so that it stands upside down, brush your base piece of paper with glue then stick it in place. Reverse the bin to stand on the base, then neatly trim off excess paper with your scalpel.

Finish your bin by applying 3 coats of varnish to lessen the chance of unwanted scratches.

Torn Paper Heart Box

THIS DELICATELY COLOURED and patterned creation shows how paper and paint – and a little know-how – can transform a plain wooden box into a decorative container fit to grace any mantelpiece. The different coloured papers – some treated with tea and bleach for added appeal – have been torn into soft hearts and squares. Once the perfect design has been arranged, the squares and hearts are gently glued into place, then the whole box is coated with layers of a clear satin varnish for protection. The combination of regular design with irregular shapes is always pleasing.

A beautiful box such as this is a fitting repository for the more treasured things in life – such as letters and mementos – though it can also hold the more mundane ephemera of modern living. Whatever it contains, it will have an appeal all of its own, not least because of the air of mystery that always surrounds a closed box and its unknown contents.

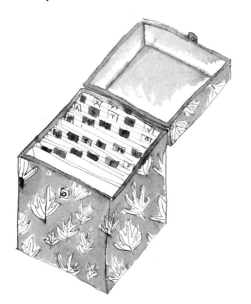

LEFT *This Torn Paper Heart Box is surprisingly simple to make, and the colourful result makes a sophisticated vessel that is both decorative and useful. Its hinged lid makes it a most appealing index card holder, and whether used in this functional way, or filled with sentimental tokens, this charming box will captivate all who see it.*

ABOVE *A stack of paper-decorated boxes – some with abstract designs, others decorated with hearts and leaves – can be put to use to hold a lifetime's treasures, or left to stand unused but glorious in an otherwise empty corner of a room.*

YOU WILL NEED

MATERIALS

1 cm/½ in thick MDF cut as follows:
*   for the base:*
*   2 of 22 x 13 cm/9 x 5¼ in*
*   2 of 20 x 13 cm/8 x 5¼ in*
*   1 of 22 x 22 cm/9 x 9 in*
*   for the lid:*
*   2 of 22 x 7 cm/9 x 2¾ in*
*   2 of 20 x 7 cm/8 x 2¾ in*
*   1 of 22 x 22 cm/9 x 9 in*
*   + an offcut*
White household glue · car body filler ·*
white emulsion · pink, yellow and
turquoise cold water fabric dyes · 3 tea
bags · bleach · cartridge paper · clear
satin varnish · hinges and catch

TOOLS

Masking tape · sandpaper and block ·
two 2.5 cm/1 in paintbrushes · palette ·
artist's brush · nylon brush · bradawl ·
screwdriver

* Despite not being designed for use
with wood, car body filler is perfect for
filling imperfections in wood. It dries
very quickly and can be sanded down to
a smooth finish.

1 Lay the 4 sides of the box in a straight line. Place the wood offcut between the pieces, as shown, to create a uniform gap. Tape with masking tape, then fold the pieces into the box shape so that the 20 cm/8 in lengths sit inside the 22 cm/9 in lengths. Fill any imperfections in the MDF with car body filler, and sand down when dry to a smooth finish. Check that the bottom fits neatly on top, then unfold the sides and brush neat glue on the joins, before reassembling and taping in place. Run a small trail of glue along all 4 edges of the box and place the bottom on carefully; leave to dry for 2 hours with a weight on top. Repeat for the lid.

2 Paint the box and lid inside and out with diluted glue to seal it. After leaving for a few minutes to dry, paint the box and lid inside and out with white emulsion. Leave to dry.

3 Create different colours by mixing your inks, adding water to lighten, then paint them on to sheets of cartridge paper. Don't aim for even application: the variations of shade will add to the final effect. Use tea and bleach (see p.15) to create unusual effects.

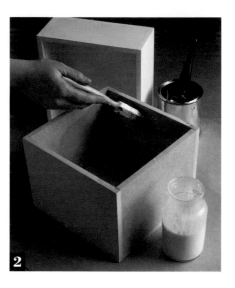

4 When thoroughly dry, tear the paper into rough squares and hearts. Again, don't aim for precision because the soft edges and the irregularity of the shapes are part of their appeal. Move the pieces around, using many different combinations, until you have a design that pleases you. The only thing to try to avoid is an imbalance of colour (e.g. all the orange squares on one side).

5 With a stronger glue solution (1 part glue to 2 parts water), apply your coloured squares of paper, and then your hearts, painting the back of each piece with a brush, then sticking on gently and smoothing out any air bubbles by hand. Alternate between the base and the lid, allowing each side to dry before placing it on the worktop.

6 Apply 2 thin coats of varnish, allowing each coat to dry, then attach the hinges and catch using a screwdriver, making holes for the screws with a bradawl.

BELOW *Variations on a theme: some of the fascinating combinations of torn paper hearts and squares.*

Autumn Leaf Tray

THIS TRAY beautifully complements the earthenware shown with it here. Amongst the strong autumnal flavours, the tray has varied leaves: some having the appearance of floating gently to the ground, whilst others boast extracts from a musical score.

Any thin papers can be used for the leaves, and their rough, sketch-like simplicity gives them an ethereal quality. The raw sienna colouring on the wood provides a gentle background for the olive green, brown and terracotta paper leaves.

If you can find a set of trays that fit into each other, Russian-doll style, why not incorporate them into a theme, such as trees, leaves and flowers on each of the separate pieces. Alternatively, if you fancy adding leaves to other objects instead of – or as well as – the tray, you could use them as decoration for the Torn Paper Heart Box (see p. 42) or the Celebration Photograph Album (see p. 30).

*Lift up any of the cups and saucers on this autumnal tray
and you will reveal a brightly dancing leaf.*

1

YOU WILL NEED

MATERIALS

Wooden tray · white emulsion · raw sienna acrylic paint · thin papers (rice, sugar, tea-bag, etc.) · yellow, turquoise and pink cold water fabric dyes · blue and black inks · white household glue

TOOLS

2.5cm/1 in paintbrush · fine sandpaper · saucer · motifs on pp. VI - VII · Japanese paintbrush · palette · scissors · glass jar · varnish with non-stick finish

1 Paint the tray inside and out with the white emulsion and leave it to dry. Rub it down with the sandpaper to remove any rough edges and repeat the process until a satisfactory surface finish is achieved. (It is worthwhile aiming for an exemplary finish so that the tray can be wiped clean in use without snagging the cloth or trapping dirt.) Now paint the tray with watered-down acrylic paint. The strength of the mixture is far from critical, but err on the side of caution with a slightly weak solution so that additional coats can be applied to the tray,

strengthening the colour with each subsequent coat. Leave your tray to one side while you concentrate on preparing your leaves.

Tear out the 2 pages of templates on pp. VI - VII and place them underneath the various papers you are using. Because of their thinness it will be easy to see the pattern below and to trace it out with a brush. Mix 2 colour washes in olive green and terracotta (see pp. 8 – 9). Using a fine paintbrush (I have used a Japanese one), paint the outlines and veins of the various leaves on to the papers. Don't be afraid to deviate from the patterns and colours to whatever extent you see fit; after all, nature never makes any 2 items identical. Paint plenty of leaves, with the expectation of having some left over.

2 Now prepare your leaves for placing on the tray. Cut out some of the shapes accurately with scissors, and rip out others quite roughly, leaving a large border of paper around them. Lay less than half of them out over the top of the tray, and decide on an arrangement you like. Don't be afraid to have leaves bending round corners. Now stick them down using diluted glue. Rotating the tray as you stick the leaves on helps to keep them reasonably evenly spaced without any particular bias to one point. Allow the glue to dry, then turn the tray over and repeat the process for the bottom and external sides of the tray.

3 When the leaves are dry, coat your tray inside and out several times with varnish to protect your work from a tumbled cup of coffee.

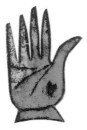

CLOCKS

ANY SHOP-BOUGHT CLOCK will tell you the time in an efficient manner, but these ingenious and fascinating clocks will do much more besides: they will intrigue and amuse you with their unusual form and stylish embellishment.

Enliven your bathroom with a clock decorated with seaweed and a starfish gleaned from a seaside stroll, and perhaps make another for the hallway, using leaves and twigs for decoration. Choose unusual decoupage motifs or opt for bejewelled numbers and silver filigree hands for a sumptuous decadent look. Whichever clock you decide to make, the result will be more than just a timepiece – it will be a masterpiece.

ABOVE *Draw your own motifs for the 'numbers', or simply use those given on pp.VIII - XI of the template section.*

Seashore Clock

CHILDHOOD MEMORIES of coastal holidays inspired the marine theme of this novel clock. Many hours spent totally absorbed in scouring the flotsam and jetsam can be so rewarding, particularly if one discovers something that bears evidence of the relentless power of the tides and that invokes memories of sea creatures trapped in rock pools, waiting patiently for the arrival of the next incoming tide.

Despite the saturated colours, from the burnt orange to the lilac, washed into the wood veneer, and the glittering surround to the clock face itself, this seashore clock has a gentle sun-bleached look to it. The stained clock face, the distressed metal leaf and the roughly torn nature of the papers all lend credence to the idea that this clock is as natural and time-worn as the beach itself.

Let hours pass by as you gaze at the collection of hand-picked aquatic treasures, culminating in a blend of tide and time.

If your passion is more for the sea than the sand, then opt for aquamarine shades and paper torn in waves to remind you of the ceaseless movement of the sea and all its water-borne treasures.

YOU WILL NEED

MATERIALS

*Rectangular piece of wood 33 x 23 cm/
13 x 9 in · white emulsion · yellow and
pink cold water fabric dyes · blue ink ·
crêpe paper · wood veneer paper (comes
on a paper backing) · 3 tea bags · clock
face (on p. VIII) · white household glue ·
1 sheet transfer metal leaf · tube of
multi-purpose glue · starfish/coral/
seaweed, etc. · clock mechanism, hands
and battery (see p. 64)*

TOOLS

*Electric drill · 2.5 cm/1 in paintbrush ·
fine grade sandpaper · saucers · artist's
brushes · scissors · jar*

1 Mark a hole one third of the way
down the piece of wood, in the
centre, then carefully drill a hole there.
Paint the wood with white emulsion on
one side and around the edges. Allow to
dry then paint the other side. (If you are in
a hurry, insert 4 pins into the painted side,
turn the wood over so that it rests on its 4
pin 'legs', then paint the second side.
Both sides can then dry simultaneously.)
Sand the painted wood down gently to
remove any gritty residue.

Use the pink and yellow fabric dyes
(just touch your brush into the powder
then stir it into a little water), and also
create purple and lilac by adding varying
amounts of blue ink to the pink dye (see
pp. 8 – 9). Wash these over the veneer and
crêpe papers. Photocopy and cut out the
clock face on p.VIII and tint it with a wash
of strong tea (see p. 15).

2 Cut and rip the prepared papers and lay them out on the wood until you are satisfied that you have reached the required design. Bear in mind when sizing the papers that the crêpe paper will expand widthways about threefold when wetted and stretched. (The yellow crêpe paper used here has already been stretched and glued in place.) I haven't worried about shaping the edges of the papers to meet each other perfectly – a slight overlap between the different papers is indiscernible.

Coat the back of one of the pieces of paper with diluted glue and stick it on to the wood in the desired place. Repeat successively with each piece of paper. Any crêpe paper used should be wetted with the glue on one side and should be lifted and stretched as it is applied. When it is in place, use the pasting brush to push the crêpe paper firmly down and avoid air bubbles. When you are sticking the wood veneer papers it is imperative that no glue finds its way on to the front side. Clean, dry fingers, together with a little care, should help you towards a flawless finish, though a dry tissue will wipe away most mistakes. Leave to dry for half an hour.

Lay one sheet of coloured veneer paper over the wood and rub round the edges to leave the clock shape. Cut out this backing paper and reserve.

3

3 The metal leaf was deliberately laid in a slightly haphazard fashion. Paint something approaching a square of diluted glue on to the papered board. Lay the metal leaf, still on the backing transfer, on top of the glue, overlapping the edge of the glue slightly to ensure that all the glue is covered. Peel away the transfer paper, leaving the gold behind. Run a finger over the leaf several times to enhance it with a 'distressed' appearance. Where it has slightly overlapped the edge of the glue it will just flake off. Give it half an hour or so to dry before covering the

back of the clock face with diluted glue and sticking it on with the centre over the hole. Now stick on the backing sheet to cover the reverse of the clock. Stick the final seaside touches on with a blob of the multi-purpose glue. When finally dry, push a small hole through the papers from the front and insert the clock mechanism (see p. 64 for details).

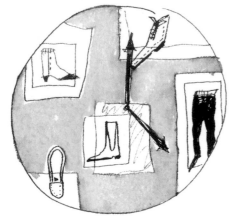

Gentleman's Outfitter's Clock

THE RATHER QUIRKY design with a sartorial flavour illustrates to an extreme the diversity of the projects that you can undertake, tailor made to either the recipient or the surroundings for which they are destined. Notwithstanding its economical appeal (it is barely possible to make a cheaper clock), it is the underlying sophistication of the idea that is the key to the success of this project. The illustrations were taken from a store catalogue dated 1895. Amongst the advertisements for carriage hardware, musical instruments, guns and sporting goods, these pictures from the millinery section particularly amused me. This catalogue (from 'the most complete store on earth') brings as much delight and instruction to us today as it did to its contemporary readers.

Such a clock can easily be themed to suit its owner: animals, flowers, books, planets, cars… the list is as unlimited as your imagination.

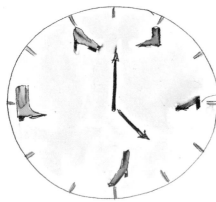

LEFT *Having mastered the basic principles, sketch out further designs, perhaps centring an idea on the theme of a favourite hobby. A clock for a keen gardener could feature leaves and flowers, or perhaps slugs and snails and other pests, as a reminder of work still to be done.*

RIGHT *Stand your hat with pride next to this rather surreal clock, choosing colours and motifs to suit the surroundings. The masculine air of this clock makes it the perfect foil to the sensuous Bejewelled Silver Clock shown on p.60.*

YOU WILL NEED

MATERIALS
*Mount board 71 x 58 cm/28 x 23 in ·
double-sided sticky tape · brown paper
25 cm/10 in square · black marker pen ·
2 sheets cartridge paper · pink and
yellow cold water fabric dyes · motifs
from pp.VIII · 3 tea bags · clock
mechanism, hands and battery
(see p. 64)*

TOOLS
*Compass · pencil · scalpel · scissors ·
drawing pin · coarse and fine grade
sandpaper · artist's paintbrush · saucer
or palette*

1 Mark two 35 cm/14 in diameter
circles and one 23 cm/9 in diameter
circle on the mount board using a
compass. With a scalpel, cut out the
circles. Cover the white side of one of the
larger circles with double-sided tape and
then trim (see p.18). Peel off the backing
paper, place the other large circle on top
(white sides together) and press firmly
together. Push a drawing pin through the
centre of the double and single circles to

leave a mark for later use. Tidy up the
edges with sandpaper.
   With the exception of a small section
about the size of a thumbprint around the
mark in the middle, cover the white side
of the smaller card with double-sided
tape. (This small gap makes inserting the
clock mechanism much easier.)

2 Peel off the shiny protective paper
and stick the brown paper on,
starting at one side, keeping it taut with
the palm of one hand. Trim off the
overlapping paper and tape with scissors
or a scalpel.
   Paint around the sanded edges of both
circles using a black marker pen.

3 Wash the cartridge papers with the
fabric dyes, both singly and in
combination. When they are dry rip out 4
rough 'squares' of different colours.
Photocopy the motifs provided on pp.VIII -
IX, tea stain them (see p.15) and cut them
out roughly, then lie them on a piece of
paper. Apply double-sided tape to the
back of the motifs, overlapping on to the
sheet of paper to ensure all the edges are
covered. Then cut out the motifs either
with or without a surround.

4 When you have achieved your
desired design, apply double-sided
tape to the coloured shapes, remove the
backing and then press them firmly on to
the small circle. Now remove the backing
paper from the motifs and press these into
position too.
   Put 4 small pieces of double-sided tape
on the back of the circle behind the
motifs, then remove the backing paper
and gently press the circle on to the large
circle, lining up centres by using a drawing
pin through the centre holes. Attach the
clock mechanism (see p.64).

3

Bejewelled Silver Clock

GLITTERING AND SENSUOUS, this clock could have been inspired by fairy tales. With rich and powerful medieval colourings, it has a magical appeal, using glass to catch the light and play tricks upon it. Any colour scheme can be used in this design.

YOU WILL NEED

MATERIALS
*Mount board 71 x 58 cm/28 x 23 in ·
double-sided sticky tape · pink cold
water fabric dye · blue ink · wood
veneer paper · aerosol adhesive ·
7 sheets transfer silver leaf · clock face
on p.IX · jewels · clear-drying general
purpose adhesive · clock mechanism,
hands and battery (see p. 64) · 2 sheets
transfer metal leaf*

TOOLS
*Large compass · drawing pin · scalpel ·
artist's brush · coarse and fine grade
sandpaper*

1 Mark two 35 cm/14 in diameter
circles and one 23 cm/9 in diameter
circle on the mount board using a
compass. Cut out using the scalpel. Cover
one side of one of the larger circles with
double-sided tape and then trim (see
p.19). Peel off the backing paper, place
the other large circle on top and press
firmly together. Push a pin through the
centre of the circles.

Leaving a small square around the
centre mark, cover one side of the large
circle with double-sided tape.

Paint the veneer paper with a purple
wash mixed from some ink and a little of
the dye powder (see p.8). Allow to dry.

2 Trim the double-sided tape on the
large circle. Place this circle on the
veneer paper and cut round the edge with
a scalpel.

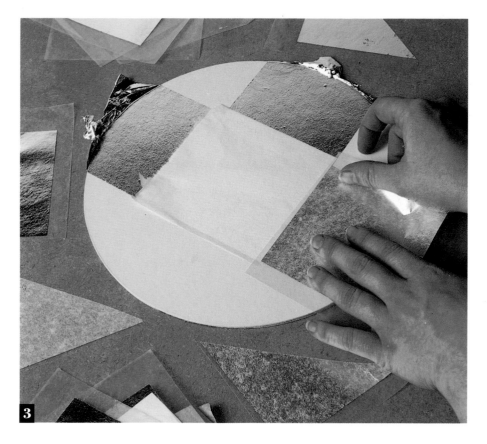

3 Peel off the double-sided backing and gently lay/roll the veneer paper on to the circle (this is best described as the reverse action of peeling off paper), using one hand to keep the paper taut and smooth out any air bubbles. Sand round the edges of both circles to tidy up the inevitable nicks and bumps left from cutting out.

Spray the reverse of 1 sheet of silver leaf and position it carefully in the centre of the clock. Leave the backing paper on to protect this sheet whilst you spray and position the 4 other sheets needed to make the cross design, as shown. Cut 2 of the silver leaf sheets in half diagonally to form 4 triangles and use these to complete the covering. A slight overlap is desirable, but not imperative, with any small character-building gaps disguised somewhat by the white background upon which they are mounted! Should you make any mistakes it is futile to try to reposition the leaf. Wait for it to dry and try again on top with a fresh piece.

4 Photocopy the numbers from p.IX of the templates section. Place your large jewels over the 3, 6, 9 and 12, then cut out round the jewels with scissors. Trim until no white paper sticks out. Then use the general purpose adhesive to glue the numbers to the clock face, and then the jewels on top.

5 Cut 8 small squares slightly larger than the small jewels from a sheet of metal leaf. Spray them with adhesive and mount them on to the clock in the positions of the vacant numbers. When the metal leaf is dry, stick the jewels on top using the general purpose adhesive.

6 Cut a sheet of metal leaf into 9 x 1 cm/½ in wide strips and spray them with adhesive. Fold them around the edge of the clock and peel off the backing paper. Apply 4 small pieces of double-sided tape to the reverse of the 3, 6, 9 and 12 positions on the smaller, silver-coloured circle, then remove the backing paper and gently press the circle on to the jewelled circle. Finally, fit the clock mechanism (see below). Prop, or hang, up your work of genius and stand back to admire it!

Once you have worked through the steps of these detailed clocks you will be more than competent enough to tackle those outlined on p.65 or variations on their themes.

NOTE ON CLOCK MECHANISMS

Before buying, or mail ordering, your clock mechanism you must know the depth of your clock face. When you have assembled your card circles, or cut your wood (depending on the project), measure the depth and then make sure that the shaft of the mechanism you choose will be long enough to protrude through the clock, still allowing for the locking nut to screw on.

To insert, push the mechanism through from behind, keeping it square. Screw the locking nut on from the front of the clock and push the hands on to the shafts at 12 o'clock.

5

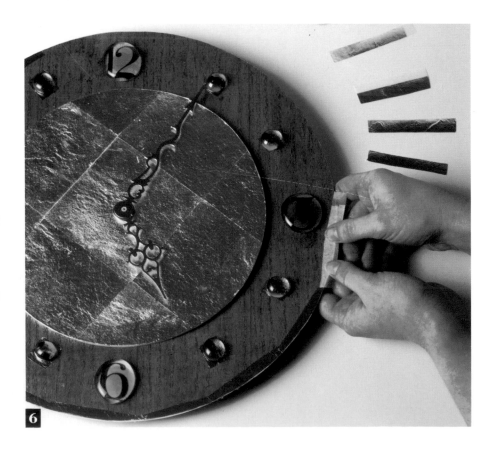

6

YOU WILL NEED

MATERIALS
Cartridge paper · blue ink · motifs on pp.VIII - IX · turquoise, pink and yellow cold water fabric dyes · mount board · double-sided sticky tape · clock mechanism, hands and battery

TOOLS
2.5 cm/1 in paintbrush · compass · pencil · scissors · scalpel

Wash the cartridge paper with some watered-down blue ink. Use the compass to draw a circle on the paper and the mount board, and cut out both (scissors for the former, a scalpel for the latter). Photocopy the shirt motifs then wash them with colours of your choice, then cut out each one with the scissors. Stick the colour-washed cartridge paper on to the mount board using double-sided tape, leaving a gap in the middle to allow for easier insertion of the clock mechanism. Place each of the shirts on double-sided tape and place them on the clock face at even intervals. Use the compass point to pierce a hole in the centre; insert the mechanism (see p.64).

YOU WILL NEED

MATERIALS
Wood veneer paper · yellow and pink cold water fabric dyes · clock face on pp.VIII · bleach · mount board · double-sided tape · clock mechanism, hands and battery

TOOLS
2.5 cm/1 in paintbrush · palette · nylon brush · jar · compass · pencil · scissors · scalpel

Wash some wood veneer paper with a burnt orange colour wash (see p.8). Photocopy the clock face template and wash it with the same colour. Brush some diluted bleach over most of the face, using the nylon brush, then cut it out.

On the veneer paper, draw 2 large overlapping circles with the compass to form the oval shape of the clock, and cut it out. Cut out the same shape from mount board, and use double-sided tape to attach the 2 shapes (leaving a gap in the middle). Stick the face on to the paper, using double-sided tape again. Use the compass point to pierce a hole in the centre. Insert the mechanism (see p.64).

YOU WILL NEED

MATERIALS
Clock face on p.IX · black ink · bleach · mount board · aerosol adhesive · 2 sheets transfer metal leaf · clear satin varnish · double-sided sticky tape · clock mechanism, hands and battery

TOOLS
Artist's paintbrush · jar · nylon brush · scissors · compass · pencil · scalpel

Photocopy the clock face and enlarge it to your required size. Wash it in black ink. When dry, use some diluted bleach to remove the ink over the numbers. Cut out the clock face with scissors.

Use the compass to draw 2 circles on to the mount board, 1 the same size as the clock face and 1 larger by 2.5 cm/1 in or so, and cut them out with the scalpel. Spray the border area of the larger circle with the adhesive, then cover it with squares of metal leaf. Next, coat the clock hands with varnish, then cover them with metal leaf. (Leave to dry for 12 hours.)

Double-side the black clock face on to the smaller circle, then double-side this on to the larger card. Insert the mechanism.

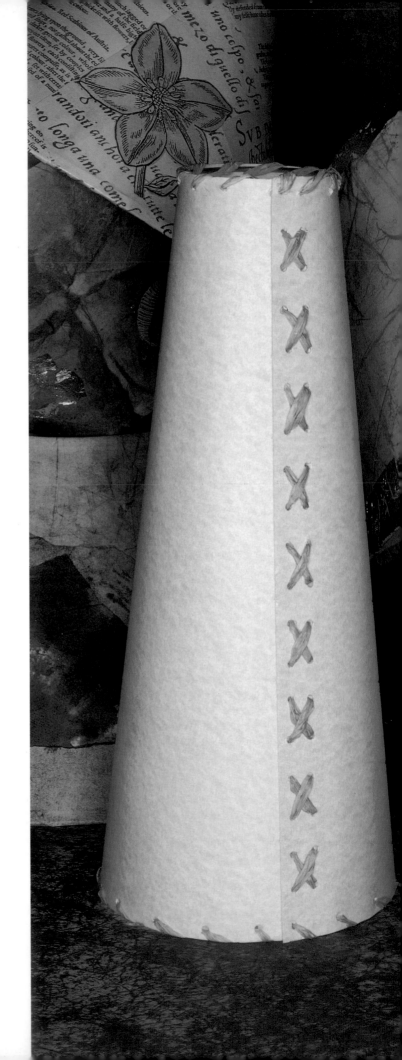

LAMPSHADES

FROM UNADORNED PARCHMENT to tea-stained copies of ancient manuscripts, there is a wide range of materials from which one can produce novel lampshades with little time and minimal guidance, and at low cost. Whilst all the shades shown here are as practical and useful as they are beautiful, some are additionally transformed when lit: the gold leaf changes from its lustrous state into a silhouette emblazoned on a textured paper, while the moths prepare to fly into the night. Useful and elegant, these pieces each invoke different moods, giving a note of muted luxury to both town and country interiors.

The textured papers used for many of these shades would almost be decoration enough, yet the addition of the metal leaf adds an undoubted finishing touch.

Stitched Parchment Lampshade

THIS GLOWING creamy yellow shade is a perfect match for the azure base and would make a focal point in any room. I chose to use parchment paper for this shade, which is decoratively stitched with raffia, and the result is a strikingly classic shade that belies its low cost and simple construction. This modern interpretation of a traditional design will match anything you can find in exclusive designerware shops – and for a fraction of the cost, of course – and will generate universal admiration.

YOU WILL NEED

MATERIALS
Parchment paper 53 x 48 cm/ 21 x 19 in · bundle of raffia · 2 copper lampshade rings: 7.5 cm/3 in and 15 cm/6 in in diameter

TOOLS
Lampshade shape from p.X · pencil · scissors · dressmaking pin · bradawl · ruler · 2 paperclips · clear adhesive tape · eraser

1 Enlarge the lampshade pattern provided on p.X of the template section until it measures 49 cm/19½ in at the widest point. Cut out the enlarged pattern and trace it onto the parchment paper. Cut out your lampshade very carefully with scissors.

2 Puncture the parchment, first with the pin then bradawl, at 2 cm/¾ in gaps, 6 mm/¼ in down from the top, and at 2.5 cm/1 in gaps, 6 mm/¼ in up from the bottom. Draw 3 light pencil lines on one edge, 8 mm/⅓ in apart (8 mm/⅓ in, 16 mm/⅔ in and 2.5 cm/1 in in from the

edge). Curl the parchment to overlap the edges to the 2.5 cm/1 in mark; secure at the top and bottom with clips, and in the middle with tape. Starting 2.5 cm/1 in down from the top, pierce the parchment at 2 cm/¾ in intervals along the first two lines, stopping 2.5 cm/1 in from bottom.

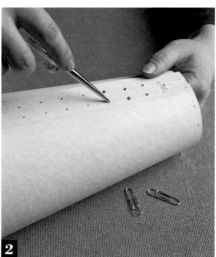

3 Cut off a 60 cm/24 in length of raffia, and tie a small knot in one end, leaving about 5 cm/2 in spare. Fix the small copper ring just above the row of holes at the top of the shade with clear tape. Starting at the hole nearest the leading edge, thread the raffia through from inside the shade up to the knot, loop over the top and back out through the next hole. Continue round and finish off by tying a knot.

For the vertical seam, tie the end of a new length of raffia (120 cm/48 in) to the 5 cm/2 in tail left at the top, then thread outwards through the top left-hand hole. Go diagonally downwards to the next hole, into the shade, then thread outwards through the top right-hand hole, and finally diagonally down to the last of the four holes to form an X. Thread down to the next group of 4 holes and repeat the process, finishing at the

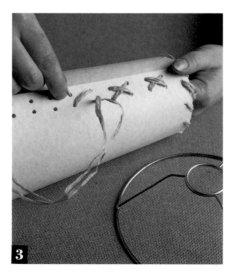

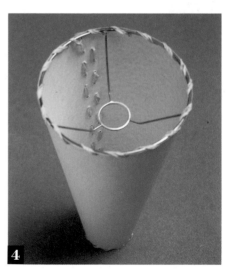

bottom of the shade with a knot. Stitch the bottom ring to the shade using the same threading technique as the top, though this time there is no need to leave a 5 cm/2 in tail.

4 The neatness of the stitching ensures that the shade looks as good from the inside as it does from the outside – however bright your bulb!

Lepidopterist's Delight

MOTHS FLUTTERING around a candle flame or lamp is a timeless image of the powerful attraction of light, and the dangers we risk in flying too close to the sun. The delicacy, almost translucency, of moths makes them a highly suitable subject for a lampshade, where the light shining through reveals their intricate form and suspends them in time and space.

The antique look to this shade is achieved by staining the covering paper – and most particularly the moth motifs – with some very strong tea. A selection of detailed and beautiful moths is provided on p.XI of the template section ready for you to photocopy and use. Once the moths are in place and the paper stained there is little left to do except cut out the lampshade shape and carefully glue it to your existing shade – a plain and inexpensive shop-bought one. The chic result belies its very simple construction and modest cost and will itself become a source of attraction – of admirers of your work.

LEFT *Moths seduced by the light are the theme for these matching shades.*
RIGHT *This idea can be developed further to incorporate old depictive scenes or decorative etchings.*

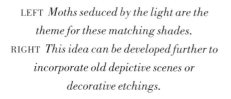

1

YOU WILL NEED

MATERIALS

Lampshade · cartridge paper (as wide as the lampshade's height and as long as the lampshade's bottom circumference) · aerosol adhesive · 3 tea bags · scissors · white household glue

TOOLS

Pencil · ruler · cup · bowl · 5 cm/2 in paintbrush · artist's paintbrush · jar

1 Lay the shade with the seam facing down on a piece of cartridge paper and roll it right round, marking a pencilled curve a finger's width from each edge in enough places to subsequently draw an outline from which to work. These marks needn't be too exact since they will be trimmed later. At each end allow about 1 cm/½ in for the seam to overlap. Join the ends of the curves where the seam will be with a ruler and pencil. Join up the marks freehand to produce the curves as shown. Photocopy the moth templates on p.XI. Enlarge or reduce them as you wish. Rip out the moths and place them on the paper within the lines, using aerosol adhesive to keep them in place. Avoid placing them too close to the edge if you don't want them trimmed (try to remember which finger you used for marking the shade!). Take a copy (or several, for safety's sake) of the layout.

2 Brew up some tea, using 3 tea bags to a cupful of water, and stew it until it is far from drinkable. Decant into a bowl for ease of use, then wash the whole sheet of paper with the tea mixture using the larger paintbrush. Once the paper is dry give all the moths a little extra bit of staining with a finer brush, darkening them a touch more than the background. Allow to dry and cut out the lampshade shape inside the pencil lines, ensuring the seams have straight edges. Try it on the shade and ensure the seam will be parallel, trimming the ends as necessary.

3 Wash the larger paintbrush, then use it to paint the plain side of the paper and outside of the shade with some diluted glue. Roll the shade on to the paper, lining up the straight edge with any seam on the shade. Smooth out any bubbles as you go. The paper should be well soaked and will therefore need careful handling. (If you have some spare photocopies it may be worthwhile experimenting to see how well soaked the paper can be before it starts to disintegrate.) Leave to dry.

4 When the paper is dry, snip several dozen times around the lower edge, cutting no further up than the finger's width of excess paper allowed. Now glue the snippets with neat glue and carefully fold each one around to the inside of the shade, remembering that the paper is still wet and therefore needs gentle handling to avoid it tearing. Tuck each piece behind the wire frame of the shade with a fingernail to make a neat and professional finish. Repeat for the top. A little extra glue can be used if things start to dry out too quickly.

Flecked and Gilded Lampshade

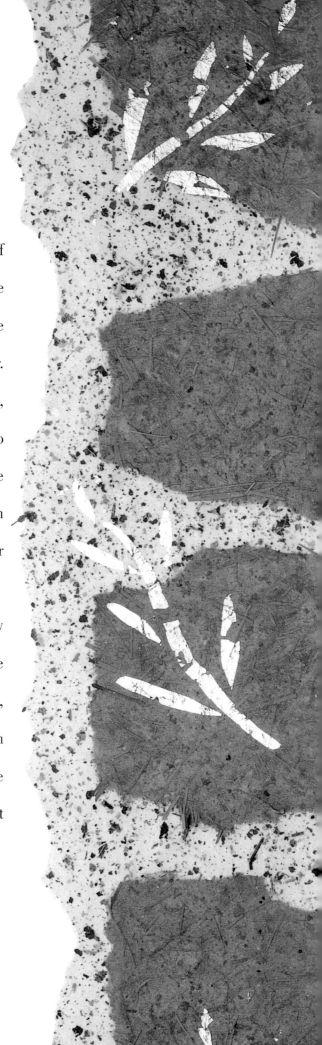

THIS ROUGH-FLECKED shade in speckled mint and olive green shows off to great effect the different qualities of the papers used to make it. The overall ground-pepper-like patterning of the minty paper offsets the wonderful rough texture and uneven finish of the olive straw paper. Whilst the combination of these two handmade papers is very effective, you can of course choose different papers for your own shade. (Buy two sheets of each paper just in case something goes wrong, or your shade is too big to fit on one sheet. The cream paper can be joined with an almost invisible seam, and because of the torn design of the green paper it does not matter how many sheets are involved.)

The design is very simple to effect and calls for no artistic ability whatsoever. The simple folding and tearing of paper produces the pattern, and it is this simplicity which gives the shade its charm, allowing the beauty of the papers to speak for itself. And whether seen unlit in daylight or lit at night, with a warm light glowing through the gaps and the gilded leaves shown in silhouette, this is a most contemporary, yet also highly sophisticated, lampshade.

This chic and subtle shade involves no more than tearing and sticking different papers - but to eye-catching effect.

This close-up of the finished shade shows the superb textural qualities of the papers.

YOU WILL NEED

MATERIALS
Plain lampshade · 2 sheets each of 2 handmade papers, each as wide as the lampshade's height and as long as the lampshade's bottom circumference · white household glue · 1 sheet transfer metal leaf · varnish

TOOLS
Pencil · ruler · scissors · jar or small bowl · 5 cm/2 in paintbrush · 2.5 cm/1 in paintbrush

1 Lay the shade with the seam facing down on the mint flecked paper. Roll the shade back and forth on the paper, confirming that the paper is sufficiently large to wrap once around the shade. With a pencil, mark a starting point at one side of the piece of paper, place the shade's seam on this, then roll it right round until the seam is back on the paper, tracing the outline which the edges of the shade follow. This is best done using a succession of consecutive marks and then joining them for the curves, adding a 'hem' of 2.5 cm/1 in at top and bottom. Use a ruler for the straight lines at the seam, again adding a margin of 2.5 cm/ 1 in. Check to see if it fits properly when wrapped around the shade, trimming the seam using a straight edge if necessary to ensure that the 2 edges are parallel when the paper is tightly wrapped around the existing shade.

When you are happy with the fit, use this piece as a template from which the green paper can be either cut or ripped into a similar shape. Little attention need be paid to the accuracy of this piece because it is subsequently ripped into several pieces.

Coat the shade with diluted glue, then lay the paper on top, stretching it slightly and smoothing out air bubbles as you do so. Make sure the seam is neat, and that the paper is pressed down very firmly where it overlaps. Don't worry about folding over the top and bottom edges yet. Now paint diluted glue all over the paper to saturate it. Allow to dry for half an hour. (This glue takes a little longer to dry if one of the surfaces is impermeable, such as the synthetic shade that I chose for used in this project.)

2 Fold the green paper shape in half, half again and finally a third time without any due concern for accuracy. Flatten the folded arrangement along the edges to leave a number of noticeable creases.

3 Unfold the paper, which should now have the creases spread across it, and lie it flat on the worktop. Casually tear out strips the length of each fold so that none of the creases remains. Choose any width of strip to rip out – the wider the gap between the 'wedges' on the shade, the greater the amount of light the shade will allow to escape. The gaps need not be of equal width because the spacing between the wedges can be evened out at stage 5. The strip being torn in this photograph was not much more than the width of a couple of fingers. Remove the first panel, leaving 7 in all (retaining the unwanted panel in case you make a mistake and need to use it as a replacement). If you cut, rather than ripped, out the shade shape, make sure you tear the remaining straight edge for consistency's sake. There should be no straight lines in sight. Throw away the strips, or perhaps save them for decoration on another masterpiece.

6 The leaf shapes and stem are cut freehand from the metal leaf with a sharp pair of scissors whilst still on the transfer backing. Keep the windows shut whilst doing this or your precious mineral will start to spread itself across the room. When cut, brush a thin layer of diluted glue on the area destined for the leaf. Rather than starting with the stem, try some of the foliage first, to allow for practice in applying the smaller pieces of the design. It is not terribly easy to apply, tearing with almost no provocation. The best advice to remember is to be gentle. Any attempt to reposition the leaf once it is touching the glue will prove futile. If, however, you are unhappy with it, scrape off with a fingernail immediately and apply a new piece.

4 Rip a piece of a similar width across the centre of each wedge and then assess your results. If any of the top wedges have gone to a point, you can tweak these off. Any other lumps and bumps that displease you can also be torn off: it is up to you just how irregular the edges are. Using a ruler or other straight edge for ripping the gaps in the paper is unwise as it may leave the shade looking as though perfect symmetry was intended. Although not unfeasible, such accuracy is difficult to achieve and as such is probably best not attempted. There is also a very pleasing and gentle quality to these rough edges, and a similar shade made using straight-edged shapes would have a more clinical look to it.

5 Stick the wedges on to the shade with the diluted glue. If you need to mix up a bit more don't worry too much about exact accuracy – as long as it is on the watery side of what comes out of the pot it will work!

Tidy up the top and bottom edges with a pair of scissors, trimming them to a consistent length of about 1 cm/½ in. Snip around the rim at top and bottom every centimetre or half inch. Add a little glue mixture on the inside of the snippets, fold around to the inside of the shade and tuck in behind the wire frame with a fingernail for a professional finish.

Use this leaf as a guide, but do not aim for exact replicas - each leaf should have its own character (see detail on p.75).

79

FRAMES

PAPER IS the perfect way of transforming plain wooden frames into works of art in their own right. Frames with little moulding work are the easiest to cover, but once you are familiar with the technique you can progress to moulded frames of more complexity.

Decorative script can look stunning on picture frames of any size. Here you can see it used on four different-sized frames, including some gilding work for added decoration on the larger two.

Both the autumnal-shaded stripes and crosses frame and the bleached blue frame are simple to make, and both have sufficient visual interest to be the perfect surround to a simple image.

This collection of frames, and the endless possibilities the projects suggest, show that a frame can be made to suit all tastes.

Bleached Blue Frame

TURN A CHEAP new frame, or an old frame with which you have become bored, into an elegant and simple masterpiece, at very low cost. With little more than the careful application of an ink wash and some bleach, an unappealing frame can be transformed in just a few hours, and be fit to take a prominent place in the house. Its Wedgwood-like combination of soft blue and white is endlessly appealing and very fresh in tone.

Some sheets of basic layout paper are treated with a pastel blue ink wash, then decorated with alternating blocks of vertical and horizontal bleached lines, with scarce use of a ruler to avoid too clinical a look. Any irregularities of line or spacing will either pass unnoticed or even add to the charm. Once dry, the paper is gently stretched and glued in place on the front and sides of the frame. A reverse pattern of speckled blue and white ensures a highly professional finish.

The inclusion of the simplest of pictures inside a frame works well when the frame is more than just a simple border, and this pleasingly soft-coloured creation will flatter a single image beautifully.

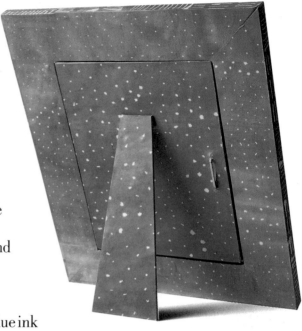

ABOVE: *The rear of the frame has a different pattern, generating added interest for admirers who choose to take a closer look at your creation. The metal bar shown on the right is used to change the pedestal for landscape use.*

YOU WILL NEED

MATERIALS

Wooden picture frame (stripped of any layers of paint or varnish, if old) · layout paper · blue ink · bleach · white household glue · clear satin varnish

TOOLS

Artist's paintbrush · scalpel · ruler · soft pencil · ruling pen · 5 cm/2 in paintbrush · scissors · eraser · 2.5 cm/1 in paintbrush

1 Brush 2 pieces of layout paper, each generously larger than the frame, with a blue ink wash composed of equal amounts of ink and water. When dry, cut one of the sheets into 4 strips, each wide enough to wrap almost right round the side of the frame, using a scalpel and ruler: 2 of the strips should be longer than the length of the frame, as shown; the other 2 should correspond to the width of the frame aperture, and thus fit between the 2 long strips (see stage 2 picture).

2 Marking very gently with a soft pencil, divide the paper strips into squares, so that there is an even number running along the horizontal borders and an odd number running down the vertical borders (in this case 2 and 5 respectively). This ensures that the patterns alternate all the way round the frame. In each square draw some guiding lines either vertically or horizontally with the pencil to ensure no irreversible mistakes in patterning order are made at the bleaching stage.

Lay the strips down and bleach across each square, following the pencilled

pattern, using a ruling pen and diluted bleach. If applied heavily, the bleach may bleed into the ink slightly – an effect being shown in the photograph. If your pressure on the pen is inconsistent so that some lines are wider than others, or even join up with the next line, do not despair: such irregularities can add to rather than detract from the final effect. Leave your paper until the bleach has had time to dry. Very gently erase the guiding pencil lines.

3 With a weak glue solution (4 parts water to 1 part glue) and the larger brush, cover the front of the frame and the back of 1 long and 2 short strips of the paper, being careful not to get glue on the front of the paper. If this does happen, you will find that the colour gets leached out of the paper. (If your fingers get glue on them, dry them.) Lay the paper on the frame, starting with the shorter sides of the frame first, then gently abut the longer strip. Spend some time stretching the papers gently to prevent them from crinkling as they dry.

Fold the paper over the outside edges of the frame and pinch the excess paper at one outside corner into a point. Cut off this spare triangle of material as close to the frame corner as you can, and remove it. The cut edges of the paper should now abut at the corner and can be folded over smoothly to the rear of the frame. Repeat for the other corner.

Now fold the paper round on the inside edges into the rebate where the glass will sit, snipping a diagonal line into each corner to allow the edges to fold over neatly.

Glue the final strip in place and follow the instructions for handling the corners. The reason for not doing both long strips at the same time is that the glue on one would dry while you were handling the corners of the other.

4 Whilst waiting for the front to dry, prepare the second sheet of layout paper for the rear by spotting it with the ruling pen and bleach mixture. Load the pen with bleach, then dot lightly over the rear of the frame until you are satisfied with the coverage. Cut the sheet into 4 strips (2 long and 2 short, as before) almost as wide as the border, plus pieces to fit the picture backing and both sides of the pedestal. Glue the strips on to the

frame with the diluted glue, covering the striped paper folded over from the front. Cover the picture backing and both sides of the pedestal in the same way. When the glue has dried, paint the whole frame with a thin coat of varnish (using the smaller brush) to give reasonable protection against wear.

Stripes and Crosses Frame

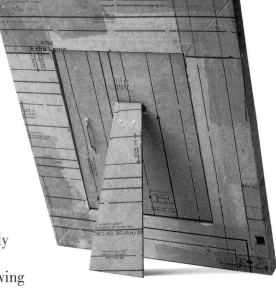

THIS SEPIA-TONED PICTURE frame is simplicity itself to make and requires very little precision. Any papers of your choice – I have opted for ones in varying shades of cream and brown – can be torn into squares with which to cover the frame, and the decoration is simply more torn paper, this time strips decorated with thin and thick ink lines, and arranged to form crosses. The result is subtle and understated, and would be equally at place in a study, or, as shown here, on a dressing table with glowing bottles to offset its gentle colouring.

The crosses were arranged without any attention to symmetry, and the random nature of the content provides a pleasing contrast to the necessarily straight and narrow form of the frame itself. You could, of course, use designs other than crosses with equally pleasing results.

ABOVE *Covering the rear of the frame adds to its appeal and gives a professional finish. The dressmaking pattern paper looks quite acceptable on its own, but if your frame will often be seen from the rear you might wish to continue the decorative scheme from the front.*

LEFT *Use any motifs as decoupage decoration for a frame – either motifs of your own or ones reproduced at the back of the book. In this way you can customize a frame by your choice of motifs, in much the same way as was suggested for the clocks on p.65.*

YOU WILL NEED

MATERIALS
Black ink · selection of papers, including dressmaking patterns · wooden picture frame (stripped of any layers of paint or varnish, if old) · white household glue

TOOLS
Artist's paintbrush · ruling pen · 2.5 cm/1 in paintbrush

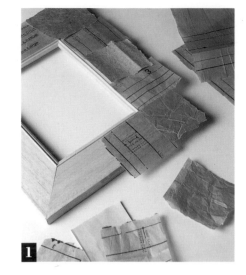

1 Mark with ink a random selection of the different papers you have chosen, using both the ruling pen and the artist's brush, depending on the thickness of the line required. To mark a contrast with the perfectly straight lines on any dressmaking or tailoring patterns you may be using, try to avoid using a ruler on any plain pieces of paper. Rip some of the papers into squares wide enough to cover the front of the frame and wrap around the outside edge to the rear. Rip other bits into strips of varying thicknesses, and use these to form the crosses.

2 Lay all the rough squares on to the frame, overlapping the edges just a little, until the frame is covered. I have chosen an even arrangement of these squares to form lines of 5 and 2, but you could have smaller or larger squares or an uneven number. Now add the crosses, and arrange and rearrange the squares and crosses in as many different combinations as it takes to find the most pleasing arrangement. The crosses can be used singly or in twos.

3 Using diluted glue, coat some of the thicker papers on the reverse side. The heavier the paper, the more soaking it will need. There is no need to coat the back of the tissues. Coat about a quarter of the frame on the front and outside edge, and then stick the squares on, folding around on to the back, stretching the papers gently as you do so. The overlaps of each paper will be hardly discernible if you smooth them over carefully. Paste on the crosses then leave to dry for 30 minutes.

4 The reverse of the frame can be covered with a less complex design. Here I have used squares of tailoring paper on the frame itself, and sheets of the same on the picture backing and pedestal. A mount board (shown here uncut) from which a rectangle is cut with a scalpel and ruler will greatly enhance whatever picture is placed in the frame.

BELOW *Some of the endless combinations of squares and crosses you can achieve by varying patterning and relative sizes.*

Gilded Script Mirror

A BEAUTIFUL AND delicately gilded frame such as this may soften the blow of meeting your reflection in the bathroom mirror every morning. The glass itself cannot lie, of course, but you could easily be forgiven for gazing admiringly at what surrounds the mirror if the truthful image in the centre does not inspire you in quite the same way!

YOU WILL NEED

MATERIALS

3 tea bags · circular piece of MDF 45 cm/18 in diameter · white emulsion · white household glue · circular mirror 25 cm/10 in diameter · 3 sheets transfer metal leaf · two-part epoxy glue or contact/impact adhesive

TOOLS

Documents or scripts from p.XII · saucer · artist's brush · sandpaper · scissors · jar · 2.5 cm/1 in brush · pencil

1 Photocopy some of the scripts supplied on p.XII, or use your own documents, making the most of any enlarging or reducing facilities the copier may have. Perhaps enlarge a favourite piece of text or pattern repeatedly, feeding successive copies back on to the glass for extra enlarging. Then, using the artist's brush, give all the papers a strong wash of tea (see p.15) with no particular regard to uniformity of application.

Smooth off the edges with sandpaper and paint both sides and the edge of the MDF circle with white emulsion, leaving it for half an hour or so until dry to touch. This is probably best done in two successive stages.

2 Lay out the papers, cutting and trimming them as necessary. Overlap the papers so that none of the white board can be seen. Remember to allow enough spare paper at the edges to wrap around on to the back of the wood.

When you are happy with the layout, brush diluted glue over the back of the paper and lay it on to the painted MDF. Try to stretch the paper outwards slightly by rubbing gently with the palms of your hands, pushing out any air bubbles at the same time.

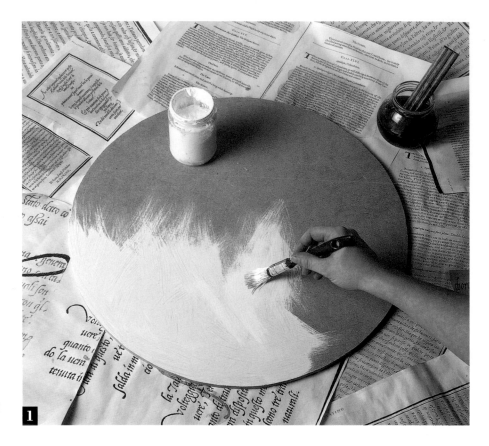

3 When the front has been covered, and the glue has dried, snip every centimetre/half inch or so around the edge with a pair of scissors. Brush more glue on to the snippets and fold them round to the back of the circle. If you have enough spare papers you can also cover the rear of the mirror. Lay the paper on the wooden circle and rub it round the edge to form a mark around which to cut. Should you not consider this back paper necessary you may want to trim the snippets to an equal length before gluing for a neat finish.

4 Position the mirror in the centre and draw round it with a pencil. Cut the metal leaf into curved strips with scissors without removing it from the backing paper. Paint the diluted glue around the circle, ensuring that some is applied just inside the circle. Lay the metal leaf on the glue and remove the backing. Try to overlap into the inside of the circle slightly. Slide a finger across each piece gently to create cracks and break the uniformity of the circle. Allow to dry.

Finally, glue the mirror itself on with a number of pea-sized dollops of a two-part epoxy or contact adhesive. Avoid putting the dollops too close to the edge so that when you put some gentle weight on the mirror it won't be forced out on to the leaf. Leave flat until the recommended drying time of the glue has been achieved.

Suppliers

UK

GENERAL
Habitat*
196 Tottenham Court Road
London WIA 1BJ
0171 631 3880
(and branches)

Heal & Son*
196 Tottenham Court Road
London WIA 1BJ
0171 636 1666

Ikea*
Brent Park
2 Drury Way
North Circular Road
London NW10 0JQ
0181 451 5566
(and branches)

ARTISTS' SUPPLIES
Diamond Suppliers
25-26 Sunbury Workshops
Swanfield Street
London E2 7LF
0171 739 6500

London Graphic Centre
Unit 9-10 McKay Trading Estate
Kensal Road
London W10 5BN
0181 969 6644
(and branches)

E. Plutons*
273 Archway Road
London
0181 348 0315

SOURCE DESIGNS
Dover Books
18 Earlham Street
London WC2
0171 836 2111

PAPERS
Falkiner Fine Paper*
76 Southampton Row
London NC1B 4AR
0171 831 1151

T.N. Lawrence & Son
119 Clerkenwell Road
London EC1R 5BY
0171 242 3534

Paper Chase*
213 Tottenham Court Road
London W1P 9AF
0171 580 8496
(and branches)

CLOCK PARTS
Maplins*
PO Box 777
Rayleigh
Essex SS6 8LR
01702 552911
(and branches)

H.S. Walsh and Sons Ltd*
12-16 Clerkenwell Road
London EC1M 5PL
0171 253 1174
also
243 Beckenham Road
Beckenham
Kent BR3 4TS
0181 778 7061

US

GENERAL
Pottery Barn
100 North Point
San Francisco CA 94133
800 922 5507

ARTISTS' SUPPLIES
Sam Flax
111 8th Avenue
New York NY 10011
212 620 3060

Sax Arts and Crafts
PO Box 51700
New Berlin WI 53151
414 784 6880

PAPERS
Andrews Nelson Whitehead
31-10 48th Avenue
Long Island City NY 11101
718 937 7100

Amsterdam Art
1013 University Avenue
Berkeley CA 94710
415 548 9663

Colophon Book Arts Supply
3046 Hogun Bay Road NE
Olympia WA 95806
206 459 2940

Color Craft
14 Airport Park Road
E. Granby CT 06026
800 243 2712

*Mail Order available

Decorative Papers
PO Box 749
Easthampton MA 01027
413 527 6103

Earth Guild
33 Haywood Street
Asheville NC 28801
800 327 8448

Paper Art Company
7240 Shadeland Station
Suite 300
Indianapolis IN 46256
800 428 5017

CLOCK PARTS

Clock Repair Center
33 Boyd Street
Westbury NY 11590
516 997 4810

Klockit
PO Box 542
Lake Geneva WI 53147
800 556 2548

Otto Frei & Jules Borel Co.
126 2nd Avenue
Oakland CA 94604
510 832 0355

SOUTH AFRICA

Art & Graphics Supplies
169 Oxford Road
(Nedbank Centre entrance)
7B Mutual Square
Rosebank
Johannesburg
011 442 9563

X-Press Graph-X
29 Siemert Road
Doornfontein
011 402 4522

Crafty Supplies
32 Main Road
Claremont
Cape
021 610 286

AUSTRALIA

Janet's Art Books Pty Ltd
143 Victoria Avenue
Chatswood
NSW 2067
02 417 8572

Handworks Supplies
121 Commercial Road
South Yarra
VIC 3141
03 820 8399

NEW ZEALAND

Gordon Harris
4 Gillies Avenue
Newmarket
Auckland
520 4466

Littlejohns
170 Victoria Street
Wellington
385 2099

Acknowledgements

Many thanks go to all the following:
Simon – my driving force, confidant and friend, and without whom this project would have been impossible;
Louise Simpson – for having the vision and confidence to allow my imagination to run free;
Alison Fenton – for making this book look fantastic and for friendship, guidance and advice;
Alison Bolus – for being endlessly patient and consistently compassionate;
Carl Warner – for translating my ideas and making the book come alive – and his assistant Sarah;
Camilla – for help with styling; Hilda and John – for endless amounts of encouragement;
Juliet – for love and support; Robert – for always being at the end of a phone.

Thanks also to the following for generously donating materials or allowing us to borrow props for use in the
photographic shoots: Absolutely; Conran Shop; Designers Guild; Falkiner Fine Paper;
Fulham Cross Antiques; Global Village; H.S. Walsh & Sons; London Graphic Centre; Paper Chase;
Papyrus Stationers; The Dining Room Shop.

Index

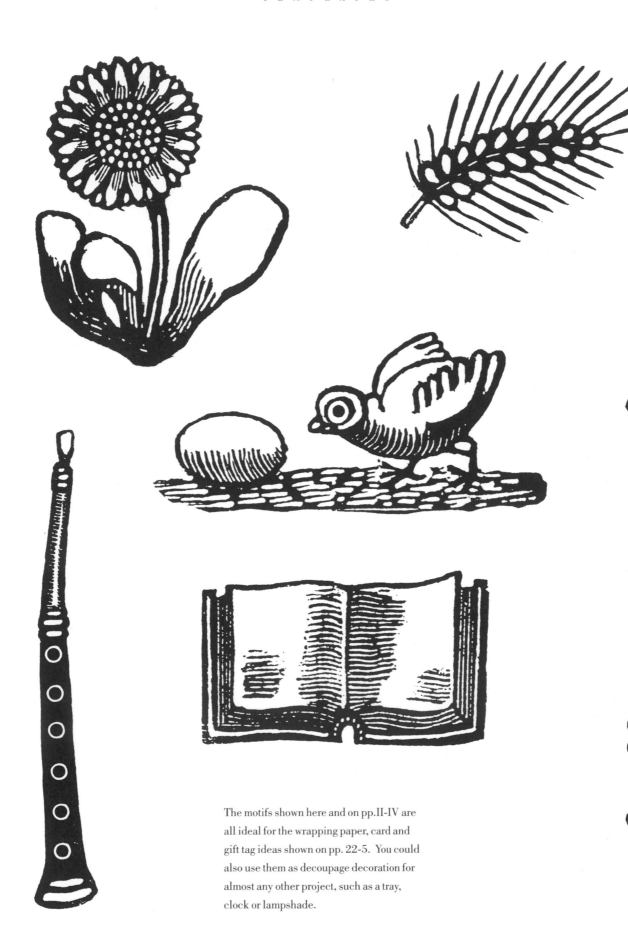

The motifs shown here and on pp.II-IV are all ideal for the wrapping paper, card and gift tag ideas shown on pp. 22-5. You could also use them as decoupage decoration for almost any other project, such as a tray, clock or lampshade.

Use these motifs at this size, or enlarge or
reduce them as you wish. Using them with a
combination of decorative paper treatments
such as colour-washing, tea staining and
bleaching will produce a wide variety of
impressive effects, and make gift wrapping
an absolute pleasure.

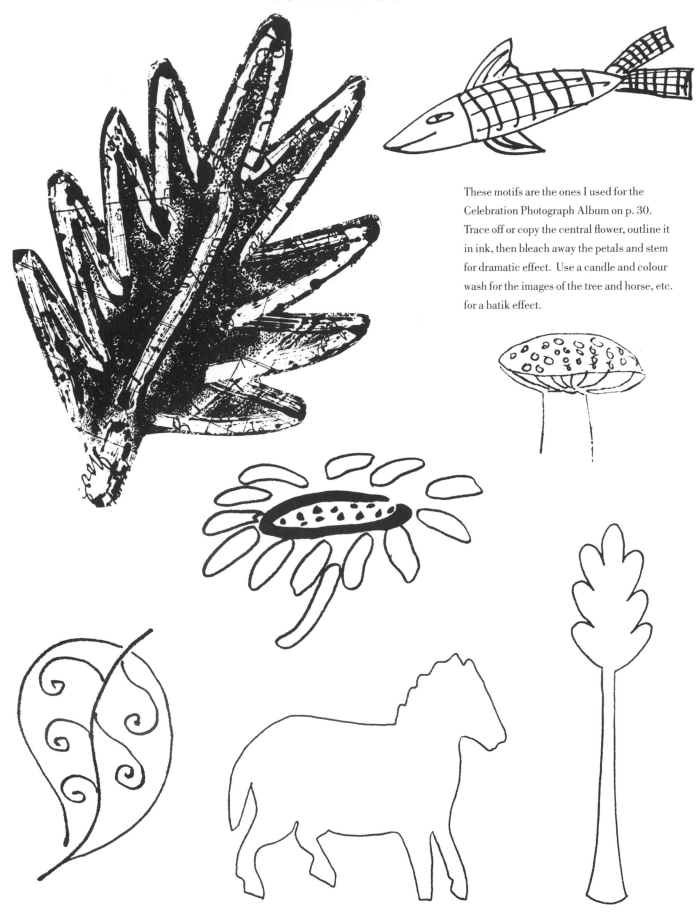

These motifs are the ones I used for the
Celebration Photograph Album on p. 30.
Trace off or copy the central flower, outline it
in ink, then bleach away the petals and stem
for dramatic effect. Use a candle and colour
wash for the images of the tree and horse, etc.
for a batik effect.

Trace the leaves on these two pages straight
on to the thin papers suggested for the
Autumn Leaf Tray. These simple decoupage
motifs will transform a plain wooden tray in
minutes, and at almost no cost. An
alternative design could include
some of the moths from p.XI as well.

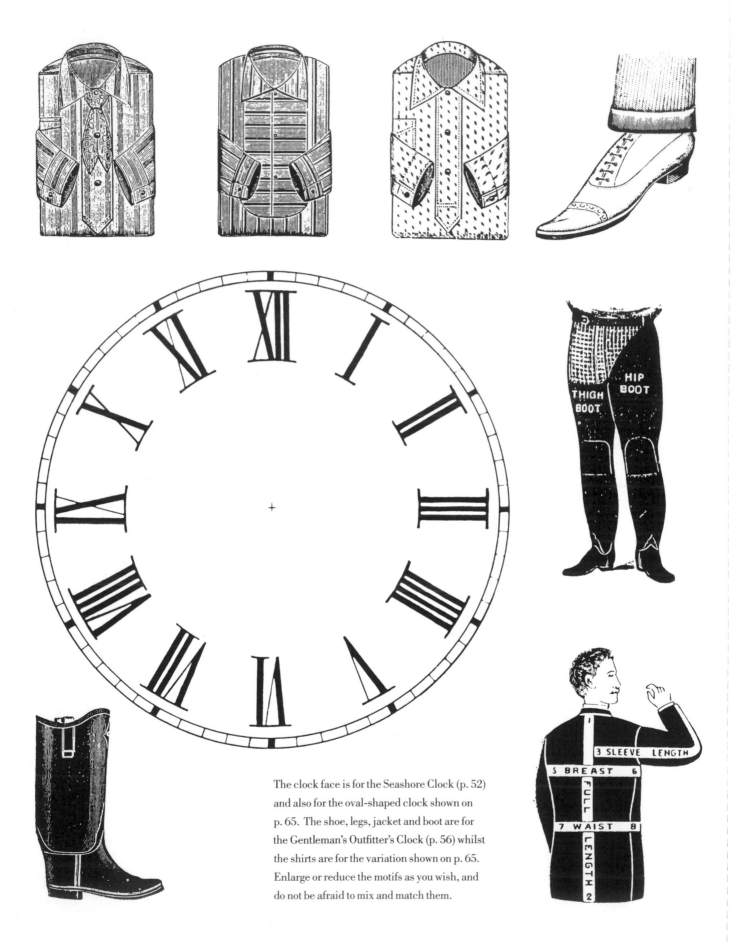

The clock face is for the Seashore Clock (p. 52) and also for the oval-shaped clock shown on p. 65. The shoe, legs, jacket and boot are for the Gentleman's Outfitter's Clock (p. 56) whilst the shirts are for the variation shown on p. 65. Enlarge or reduce the motifs as you wish, and do not be afraid to mix and match them.

You will find innumerable uses for these bold, stylish numerals. I used them for my Bejewelled Silver Clock, and also for one of the variations shown on p. 65, but they would look equally at home on all manner of clocks. The different treatments I gave them – semi-obscured behind gleaming jewels, or bleached out of a dark colourwash – are just two ideas.

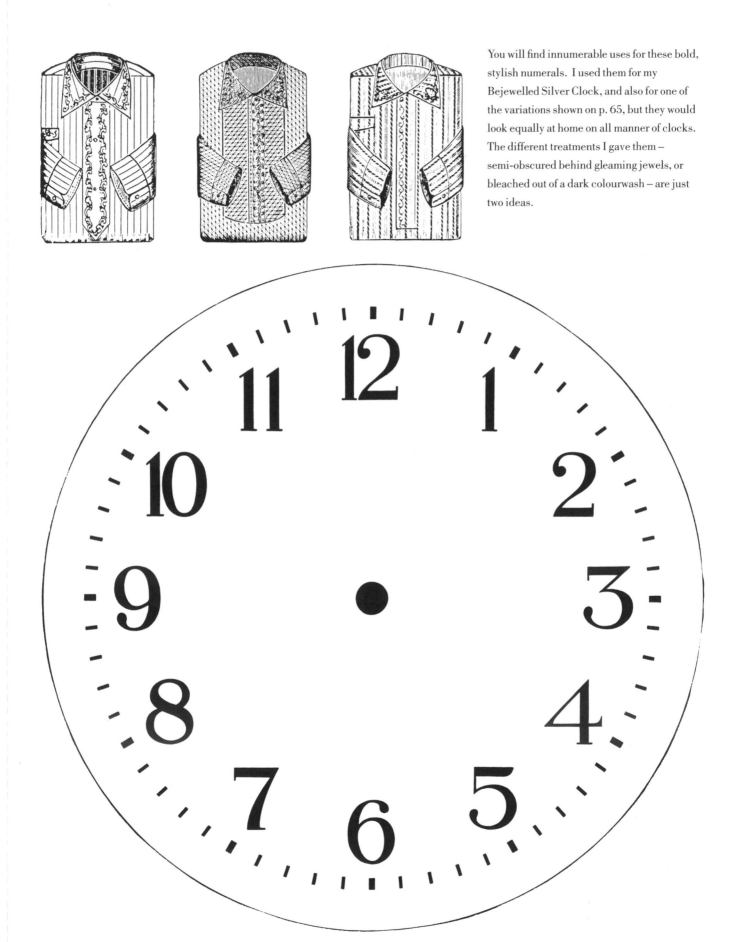

Enlarge this lampshade until it measures
24.5 cm/9¾ in at the widest point. Photocopy
it twice, then cut out both halves and stick
them together along the vertical edge to
make the final shape for the Stitched
Parchment Lampshade (p. 68).

X

These delightfully detailed moths will look very sophisticated with the tea wash treatment shown on p. 70, but you could equally well choose a colour wash, such as a moss green, for a very different, but equally impressive, effect.

224

217

226

228

215

225

218

213

212

222

208

229

These sample scripts will transform whatever you apply them to, from wastebins and trays to frames and clocks. There is something mysteriously appealing about this pen-work, particularly if it is in a language which you cannot understand! Touches of metal leaf can add a distinguished final touch.

~: Marcus Antonius Casanoua :~

Pierij vates, laudem si opera ista merentur,
Praxiteli nostro carmina pauca date'.
Non placet hoc; nostri pietas laudanda Coryti est;
Qui dicat hæc; nisi vos forsan utrop mouet;
Debetis saltem Dijs carmina, ni quoqs, et istis
Illa datis. iam nos mollia saxa sumus.

Et per darti amaestramento in ogni tuo bisogno partenente allarte del scriuere, io te dechiaro la bota delle carte perte

~: Al benigno Lettore' :~

Pregato piu uolte', anzi constretto da molti amici benignissimo Lettore, che riguardo hauendo alla publica utilita e comodo non solamente' di questa eta', ma delli posteri anchora, uolessi dar qualche' essempio di scriuere, et regulatamente' formare' gli caratteri e note' delle' lre' che (cancelaresche hoggi di chiamano) uoletier pigliai questa fatica: E perche impossibile' era de mia mano porger tanti essempi, che sodisfacessino a tutti, mi sono ingegnato di ritrouare questa nuoua inuentione' de lre', e metterle in stampa, le' quali tanto se' auicinano alle scritte' a mano, quanto capeua il mio ingegno, E se' puntualmente' in tutto no te rispondono, supplicoti che mi facci iscasato, Conciosia che' la stampa no possa in tutto ripresentarte' la viua mano, Spero nondimeno che imitando tu il mio ricordo, da te stesso potrai consequire' il tuo desiderio. ~ Uiui, e sta Sano :~

A II

La lettera antiqua tonda rechiede grande ingegno di misura, et arte. qual uolendo imparar, Prima e necessario saper far tutte Le letter del sotto scritto Alphabeto

A A B B C C D D E E F G G H H J J
K L L M M N N O P P Q Q R R S
S T T U U V V X X Y Z & & B B & B

Molte cose ci restariano da dire, quale non pongo al presente, riseruãdomi à ponerle in vn'altr'opera non meno vtile di questa, quale piacendo à Dio fra puochi mesi, mandarò fuori à commune vtilità et satisfattione di coloro che se ne dilettano.

IL FINE.

O ltra di